SMALL GOALS Big Dreams

Achieving Your Wildest Aspirations One Step At A Time

BY OLIVIA MURRAY

contents page

V. Celebrating Progress And Maintaining Momentum

VI. Moving Beyond Small Goals

VII. Conclusion

VIII. Additional Resources

Welcome Readers

"Small Goals, Big Dreams: The Power of Consistent Progress."

Welcome, dear reader! Are you tired of constantly setting big, overwhelming goals for yourself, only to feel disappointed when they don't come to fruition? Are you looking for a more effective way to achieve your dreams and reach your full potential? Look no further.

In this book, we will explore the concept of "Small Goals, Big Dreams " and the power of consistently setting and achieving smaller goals to eventually reach our biggest aspirations. We will delve into the benefits of breaking down those dreams into smaller, manageable goals or bitesize chunks, as well as the strategies and techniques for staying motivated and focused along the way.

By the end of this book, you will have a better understanding of how to set achievable goals, stay motivated, and continuously progress towards your biggest dreams, allowing you to life your very best life!

So, let's get started on your journey, shall we?

Olivia xx

The Concept Of "Small Goals, Big Dreams"

The concept of "Small Goals, Big Dreams" is centred around the idea that breaking down larger, seemingly unattainable goals into smaller, more manageable pieces can make the pursuit of those goals much more attainable. This approach focuses on setting short-term goals that are aligned with your bigger aspirations and gradually working towards them, building momentum and confidence along the way.

I want you to think of it like a staircase leading to the top of a tall building. Each step you take brings you closer to the top, and each small goal you achieve brings you closer to realising your dream. By focusing on making steady progress towards these targets, you can keep yourself driven and on track towards your ultimate destination.

"Small Goals, Big Dreams" emphasises the power of consistent progress and the importance of taking things one step at a time. It encourages you to celebrate your accomplishments and continuously set new goals to keep pushing yourself further forward. The result, which of course we all hope to achieve, is a more fulfilling and successful life, with the realisation of your dreams as the ultimate reward.

Importance Of Setting Small Goals

Setting small goals is crucial in achieving those big dreams for several reasons:

1. Breaking down larger goals into smaller, achievable chunks makes them less intimidating and easier to pursue. By focusing on the smaller steps, you can build confidence in your abilities and stay inspired.

2. Mini goals provide a clear path to progress. By regularly achieving small target, you can see your progress and feel a sense of victory, which can keep you motivated and on track.

3. Small goals help you measure your progress and adjust your approach if necessary. As you work towards your small goals, you can reflect on what's working and what isn't, and make changes as needed to keep yourself on track.

4. Small goals keep you focused and prevent burnout. By setting smaller, manageable steps, you can avoid feeling overwhelmed and maintain a healthy work-life balance.

5. They can also provide a sense of momentum and momentum can be a powerful motivator When you see yourself making consistent

progress towards your goals, it can give you the catalyst to keep pushing forward.

In short, setting small goals helps you turn your big dreams into a tangible, achievable reality. It provides you with a roadmap to success and helps you stay motivated, focused, and on track towards your ultimate destination.

Book Structure

"Small Goals, Big Dreams" will have the following structure:

1. Introduction: This section will provide a brief overview of the concept of the book and introduce the reader to the main ideas and themes.

2. Understanding the Power of Small Goals: In this section, we will explore the importance of setting small goals in achieving your dreams and examine the benefits of this approach.

3. Setting and Achieving Small Goals: This section will cover practical strategies for setting and achieving small goals, including how to plan, how to stay motivated, and how to make steady progress.

4. Overcoming Obstacles: In this section, we will discuss common obstacles that people face when pursuing their goals and provide strategies for overcoming them.

5. Celebrating Your Accomplishments: This section will emphasize the importance of celebrating your accomplishments and recognizing your progress along the way.

6. Continuously Progressing Towards Your Big Dreams: In the final section, we will bring together all of the concepts discussed in the book and provide guidance for a breakthrough towards your ambitions.

The book will include real-life examples, practical exercises, and actionable tips to help readers implement the concepts discussed. The goal of the book is to empower you to turn their dreams into a reality using these steps.

Benefits Of Setting Small Goals

Setting small goals is a powerful tool for achieving anything. Breaking down big aspirations into smaller, manageable pieces can make the pursuit of those goals much more attainable. This approach focuses on setting short-term goals that are aligned with your bigger aspirations and gradually working towards them, building determination and a will to continue onwards.

One of the biggest benefits of goal setting is give incentive. When big dreams seem too far out of reach, they can be overwhelming and demotivating. However, by focusing on the smaller pieces of your overall puzzle, you can build assurance in your own abilities and stay spirited. Small goals provide a clear path to progress, helping you stay focused and avoid distractions.

Additionally, small goals allow you to prioritise your time and energy more effectively, leading to improved productivity and a stamina. This approach provides a framework for decision-making, allowing you to channel your efforts and make choices that align with your ultimate goals. It can also track your progress and adjust your approach if necessary, helping you stay on target and avoid feeling vanquished.

Another important benefit is increased sense of accomplishment. Regularly achieving small goals provides a sense of capability and can help boost your self-esteem and confidence. Celebrating your wins and recognising your own effort along the way is a key part of the process.

Finally, setting small goals can help you develop the key habit of overall goal setting, making it easier to set and achieve future ambitions. By focusing on making steady progress towards smaller goals, you can keep yourself motivated and on track towards your ultimate destination.

In conclusion, setting small goals is an effective way to achieve big dreams and live a more fulfilling life. By breaking down big goals into manageable pieces, you can stay motivated, focused, and on track towards success.

Limitations Of Focusing On Big Dreams

Setting small goals is a critical component of this practice. It provides a trail to happiness which makes the entire concept more feasible. This approach focuses on making your plans workable one small step at a time.

Often when faced with a big decision, or one that seems too far out of reach, it can be easy to become down hearted and give up. Setting smaller realistic goals prepares you for tackling the later trials and tribulations you may face, helping you follow your intuition and come to a resolution.

Another key benefit of setting smaller goals is improved personal efficiency. By utilising the opportunity to face one task at a time, you can hit it with full force and come out on top.

Studies have shown that even something as simple as revising for an examination it better tackled by taking small chunks of information and allowing each one to be absorbed or dealt with one at a time. The same principals apply when it comes to setting yourself a goal. Giving yourself the opportunity to take one step at a time will allow you to tackle to task with full force.

Successful People

There are many examples of successful people who have utilised the power of this technique.

One such example is Oprah Winfrey. Oprah started her journey to success as a young, struggling journalist. Instead of being discouraged by the long road ahead, she focused on setting small goals that would help her make progress towards her dream of becoming a successful media personality.

Oprah started by setting goals for herself in her current role, such as improving her writing skills and working harder to stand out from her peers. She also made a point of networking and building relationships with people who could help her advance in her career. By focusing on these small steps, she was able to build her reputation, paving the way for her eventual success as one of the most influential media personalities of our time.

Another example of a successful person who is a known goal setter is Elon Musk. Musk is a visionary entrepreneur who has achieved incredible success in several industries, including electric vehicles, space exploration, and sustainable energy. Despite his many successes, Musk has always been focused on seeing the bigger picture through a smaller lens.

For example, when Musk founded Tesla, he set the assignment of producing a high-quality electric car that could compete with traditional gasoline-powered vehicles. This goal helped him focus his efforts as he worked to build his company. Over time, as Tesla became more successful, Musk set new goals, such as expanding production and expanding into new markets. He has been able to build an incredibly successful company and make real progress towards his big dream of a sustainable energy future.

In both of these examples, it is clear that following this method works and was a critical factor in the success of these individuals. By being realistic with achievable targets and building traction, they were able to move forward and eventually to where they really wanted to be.

Assessing Your Big Dreams

 Assessing your dreams is a crucial first step in setting your mini goals. It helps you clarify what you really want to achieve and provides a foundation for the goal-setting step. To assess your dreams, you need to take a step back and reflect on what is truly important to you.

Start by thinking about your values and what kind of life you want to lead. Consider your personal interests and passions, as well as any long-term aspirations you may have. Try to get a clear picture of what your ideal life would look like, and what you would like to achieve in the future.

A great way to do this could include creating a mood or vision board. A vision board is a collage of images, words, and phrases that represent a person's goals, dreams, aspirations, and desires. It is a visual representation of what a person wants to achieve or become in the future. The idea behind a vision board is that by placing these images, words, and phrases in a prominent place, the person will be reminded of their goals every day.

Another recommendation would be to try Meditation. Meditation can be a helpful tool in aiding with goal setting because it can help clear the mind, promote focus and concentration, and reduce stress and anxiety. By meditating regularly, you can create a calm and cantered state of mind that is conducive to effective goal setting. Meditation can also help a person identify their true desires and priorities, which can be useful in creating a focused and meaningful vision for their future. Additionally, meditation can be used as a tool for visualising and manifesting your goals, helping to create a deeper connection with them and increasing the chances of successfully achieving them.

Next, you should consider your current situation and what may be holding you back from achieving your big dreams. This could include financial constraints, limited time or resources, or personal obstacles. It's important to be honest with yourself about the challenges you may face and to develop a realistic understanding of what it will take to get you where you want to be.

Once you have a clear understanding of your dreams, you can start to plan and that will help you begin the process of smashing them out of the park!

It's important to choose goals that are aligned with your ethics and ambition and that will bring you closer to the life you want to lead. When setting goals, make sure they are specific, measurable, and achievable, and set a timeline for achieving them constructively.

Making It Bitesize

Breaking down big dreams into smaller, bitesize pieces is a critical step in the goal-setting process. This approach helps you focus on making steady progress towards your ultimate aspirations, one step at a time. When you break down big dreams into smaller goals, you can focus on what you need to do today to make progress towards your big dreams, rather than becoming overwhelmed by the big picture.

When we talk about goals, we often use the term SMART. SMART is an acronym for Specific, Measurable, Achievable, Relevant, and Time-bound. SMART goals are a method of goal setting that helps to make sure that goals are clear, actionable, and realistic.

Specific: The goal must be clearly defined and well-defined.

Measurable: The goal must be quantifiable, with clear metrics to track progress.

Achievable: The goal must be realistic and within reach, given the person's current resources and abilities.

Relevant: The goal must align with the person's values, aspirations, and overall life plan.

Time-bound: The goal must have a deadline, giving a sense of urgency and motivation to work towards it.

By following the SMART method, people can ensure that their goals are clear, and well-structured.

To break down big dreams into smaller goals, start by thinking about the end goal. Ask yourself, "What will I have achieved when I have accomplished this big dream?" Once you have a clear picture of the end goal, you can start to think about the smaller steps you need to take to get there.

When setting smaller goals, make sure they are specific, measurable, and achievable.

For example, instead of simply saying: -

"I want to become a successful businessperson,"

Set a specific goal such as: -

"I want to start my own business within the next two years and achieve a profit of $100,000 in the first year."

This goal is specific, measurable, making it a clear and motivating target to work towards. You could even break this down further into more manageable steps. Let's face it we all love the satisfaction of getting things done. So, make your goals tiny fragments of what you hope to achieve overall. It will give you a boost each time you check something off that to do list for sure!

It's important to prioritize your smaller goals and focus on what is most important. Start by identifying the key steps you need to take to achieve your big dream and focus on these first. Then, as you make progress, you can add additional goals that build on your previous successes.

In conclusion, breaking down big dreams into smaller, achievable goals is a critical component of success. By focusing on small, manageable steps, you can stay motivated and make steady progress towards your big dreams. This approach also helps you prioritise your time and resources, ensuring that you are making the most of your efforts as you work towards your ultimate aspirations.

Prioritising And Creating an Action Plan

To prioritise your goals, start by thinking about what is most important to you and what you want to achieve first. Consider the impact that each goal will have on your life and what will bring you the most value. Focus on the goals that are most aligned with where you want to be in your immediate future and how you can then work towards your end game.

Once you have identified your priorities, it's time to create a plan of action. A plan of action should include specific steps you need to take to achieve each goal, as well as a timeline for completion. Make sure your plan is realistic and achievable, taking into consideration the time, resources, and support you have available.

Let's use the example of setting up our own business. These are just a few of the small goals you may start with in order to get your idea off the ground: -

1. Conduct market research:

   Goal: To gain an understanding of the target market and competition.

Action Steps:

- Identify potential customers and their needs.
- Research the competition and their strengths and weaknesses.
- Evaluate the potential demand for the product or service.

2. Develop a business plan:

Goal: To create a roadmap for the business and secure funding.

Action Steps:

- Define the business model and its objectives.
- Determine the target market, sales and marketing strategies, and budget.
- Create a financial plan and secure funding through loans, grants, or investors.

3. Set up the legal and administrative aspects of the business:

Goal: To ensure compliance with legal and regulatory requirements.

Action Steps:

- Register the business and obtain all necessary licenses and permits.
- Establish a tax structure and accounting system.

- Set up a bookkeeping and record-keeping system.

4. Choose a location and set up the physical infrastructure:

   Goal: To have a suitable workspace for the business.

Action Steps:

- Identify a suitable location for the business.

- Set up the physical infrastructure, including equipment, furniture, and supplies.

- Develop a plan for security and maintenance.

5. Launch the business:

   Goal: To start generating revenue.

   Action Steps:

- Develop a launch strategy and execute it.

- Start selling the product or service.

- Monitor and evaluate the business's performance and adjust as necessary.

By following this plan of action, the process of starting a business can be less overwhelming and more efficient.

It's also important to set milestones and to celebrate your successes along the way. Achieving small goals can help build momentum and keep you motivated as you work towards the finale.

Here are some suggestions for celebrating milestones in the plan of action for setting up a business:

1. Market research: Celebrate the completion of market research by treating yourself to a special activity or taking a day off.

2. Business plan: Celebrate the completion of the business plan by having a small celebration with friends, family, or business partners.

3. Legal and administrative setup: Celebrate the completion of the legal and administrative setup by taking a break or treating yourself to something special.

4. Physical infrastructure: Celebrate the completion of the physical infrastructure by having an open house or inviting friends and family to see the new space.

5. Launch: Celebrate the launch of the business by having a launch party or event, or by treating yourself to a special activity or reward.

By celebrating milestones can also help keep excitement levels high, which is essential for sustained success.

Finally, be flexible and adaptable in your approach. Life is unpredictable and things may not always go according to plan. If you encounter obstacles or setbacks, don't give up. Instead, re-evaluate your goals, adjust your plan of action, and keep moving forward.

Prioritising goals and creating a plan of action is key to you winning with you small goals and eventually those big dreams. By focusing on what is most important and developing a clear and concise actions, you can win. Celebrating your successes and being malleable in your approach will help you on the ultimate path to success.

Overcoming Obstacles And Setbacks

Overcoming obstacles and setbacks is an inevitable part of the journey towards achieving your goals and dreams. No matter how well you plan, there will be times when you encounter challenges that test your resolve and threaten to derail your progress. However, the key to success is to not let these obstacles define you and to instead use them as opportunities to grow and learn.

The first step in overcoming obstacles and setbacks is to stay positive and maintain a growth mindset. Believe in yourself and your ability to overcome the challenge. Focus on what you can control and take one step at a time towards your goal.

Next, seek support and advice from others. Talking to friends, family, or a mentor can help you gain new perspectives and find solutions to the challenges you are facing. They can also provide you with encouragement and support when you need it most.

It's also important to have a backup plan and be prepared for the unexpected. Having a contingency plan can help you quickly respond to any setbacks or obstacles and keep you moving forward.

Let's take a look at an example for our business as an example of what you may come across:-

Competition: The obstacle of competition from established businesses in the same industry. This can make it difficult to attract customers and generate revenue.

And how would you tackle this: -

Niche specialization: Instead of competing with established businesses head-on, focus on a niche area that they may not be serving. This will allow you to differentiate yourself and attract customers who are looking for something specific.

In this example by taking a proactive approach to the competition, you could increase your chances of success and attract more customers.

Finally, take care of yourself and focus on your mental and physical health. When you are feeling overwhelmed, it's easy to get caught up in the stress and negativity. However, taking care of yourself, through activities such as exercise, meditation, or spending time with loved ones, can help you stay focused and motivated.

In conclusion, overcoming obstacles and setbacks is a necessary part of the journey towards achieving what you want. By staying positive, seeking support, being prepared, and taking care of yourself, you can overcome the challenges you encounter and keep moving forward which is where you want to be!

Building A Supportive Network

Building a supportive network is a crucial aspect of achieving your small goals and big dreams. Having a network of people who believe in you, encourage you, and offer support when you need it can make all the difference in helping you overcome challenges and reach your aspirations.

The first step in building a supportive network is to identify the people in your life who align with your values and goals. This can include friends, family, colleagues, mentors, or members of a community group. These individuals should have a positive attitude and a willingness to support you on your journey.

Next, make an effort and try to develop strong relationships with these individuals. This can involve spending time with them, sharing your ideas, and seeking their advice and support. Building a network is a two-way street though, so be sure to offer support and encouragement to others in your network as well.

Another way to go about this is to seek out like-minded individuals who share your interests and goals. Joining a club, taking a class, or volunteering for a cause that you are passionate about can help you meet new people who share your values and aspirations.

Finally, it's important to use technology to stay connected with your network. Regular communication through social media, email, or video chat can help you stay in touch and offer guidance when needed.

In conclusion, building a supportive network is invaluable to achieving your success. Having a group of people who believe in you, offer wisdom and council, and share your values and ethics can provide you with the drive and determination you need to succeed.

Implementing Accountability

Implementing a system of accountability is an important and valuable step in your journey. Holding yourself accountable helps you stay focused and on track towards your destination.

The first step in implementing a system of accountability is to clearly define those goals and establish a specific timeline for achieving them. Write down your steps, along with the specific action points you need to take to make them happen and set a deadline for each one.

Next, find an accountability partner or join a support group. An accountability partner is someone who you trust and who is committed to helping you reach for the stars. They can offer support, encouragement, and help you stay on point. Joining a support group with others who have similar ideals can also provide you with a sense of community and accountability. Also a great place to vent when things aren't going so well. A good great way to get things off your chest and get your head back in the game.

Additionally, regularly track your progress and celebrate your moments, nothing better than ticking off that to do list!

Finally, be honest with yourself and hold yourself accountable for your actions. If you fall behind or encounter setbacks, don't be afraid to address them and make the relevant changes to your plan. Staying accountable and being honest with yourself is essential for long-term success, which is what we want from this process.

In conclusion, implementing a system of accountability is a crucial step in achieving your small goals and big dreams. Holding yourself accountable, finding an accountability partner or support group, tracking your progress, and being truthful can help.

The Importance Of Acknowledging Progress

Acknowledging progress is an important aspect of achieving your small goals and big dreams. It helps you stay objective, and you can clearly see when you have hit the mark.,.

First, regularly track your progress towards your goals. This can involve keeping a journal, creating a spreadsheet, using a goal-setting app or my good old favourite, just making a 'To Do' list! Tracking your development helps you see the evolution of where you have been to where you are now.

Again, I want you to celebrate your successes along the way, no matter how small they may be. This can involve rewarding yourself, sharing your progress with others, or simply taking time to give yourself a pat on the back. Any progress no matter how smal,l is a step in the right direction.

It's also important to be honest with yourself about your progress, even if it's not what you had hoped for. Take note of any setbacks or challenges you have face and use them as opportunities for growth and learning. It will enable you to make more headway letter if you come up against the same problems again.

Take the time to appreciate your evolvement and think about what you've gained from this experience. This can help you identify any areas for improvement and make changes to your plan for the future.

In conclusion, acknowledging progress is essential to achieving your small goals and big dreams. Regularly tracking your progress, celebrating your successes, being honest with yourself, and taking the time to reflect can help you stay motivated, focused, and on track towards your ultimate aspirations.

Strategies For Staying Focused

Staying on track is crucial to achieving everything your heart desires. Here are some strategies to help you maintain your spark and stick with it.

First, surround yourself with positivity and support. Surrounding yourself with individuals who believe in you and your goals, and who have you back when things get tough can provide you with the courage to keep going.

Next, it is important to establish a routine and try your very best to stick to it. Having a daily routine can help you stay organised both in your home and work life. It also helps to prioritise self-care and engage in activities that bring you joy and fulfilment, after all these are the things we really should be spending out time on in this life.

Look to find support in other places too, such as external sources. This can involve reading books, magazine articles and listening to music or podcasts. Even attending events related to your goals can be a great way of giving yourself a little boost, and really get you out there in the world.

Another great tip here is to minimise distractions when you are sending time on your goal setting.

Here are some ways to do this, especially with your devices:

1. Turn off unnecessary notifications: Go to your device's settings and turn off notifications for apps that you don't need to be alerted about.

2. Use Do Not Disturb mode: Enable the Do Not Disturb mode on your devices to silence incoming calls, texts, and notifications during specific hours or during work hours.

3. Put your phone on silent mode: If you find yourself constantly checking your phone for notifications, consider putting it on silent mode or in another room when you need to focus.

4. Use apps or software to block distractions: There are several apps and software programs available that can block distracting websites and apps for a set amount of time.

5. Limit screen time: Set a specific amount of time for using your device each day and stick to it. This can help you avoid getting lost in endless scrolling and instead stay focused on the task at hand.

6. Take a digital detox: Regularly taking a break from your devices and the constant barrage of notifications can help reduce stress and increase focus.

Clutter can create a non-karmic workspace and make it difficult to find what you need, leading to lost time and decreased productivity. To create a clutter-free workspace, start by getting rid of any items that you no longer need. Next, create a system for organising your supplies and papers, such as using file folders, trays, and labels. Ensure that everything has a designated place and make a habit of putting things back where they belong after each use. Keep up this task regularly as it will help you maintain a calm and organised environment that is conducive to productivity.

Finally, another reminder to be kind to yourself. Don't be too hard on yourself if you encounter anything you may feel difficult to overcome. Taking regular breaks can help with this. Instead, try and see any issues as opportunities to try something new, a different approach which may be more successful for you next time. Try and try again, as the saying goes.

Making Necessary Adjustments

Making adjustments to your plan as needed is an important aspect of achieving your desires and it should be taken in your stride. Life, as always is very unpredictable, and it's important to understand that being flexible and adaptable is perfectly normal to get you where you want to go.

Let's take the example of driving to work, you may discover during your route that there is roadworks. They are for sure going to hold you up and you are going to be late. What would you do, turning around and head back to be? As tempting as that may be some days, the answer is you would take another route. And life is full of them.

The best way to prepare for any adjustment is simply by tracking where you are now and where you want to be. By regularly reflecting on your successes and challenges you may have already faced, it will allow you to plan ahead and make and necessary changes to your plan as you move forwards. Regular assessments can also help you identify any areas key for improvement help considerably when making your next move.

Next, be open to feedback from others. Seek out feedback from family, friends, mentors, or a support group to help you see your progress so far from a different perspective. Having this valuable asset can give you a different perspective on things and their valuable insights can also assist you make tweak to make things better, faster and possibly even smarter.

It's also important to be aware that changes in your life, such as a new job, a health issue, or a personal setback can all take a toll on your hard work. Whether it be a direct impact on your goals themselves or simply on the time you can manage to spend on those goals. Don't feel guilty if you have to put everything on hold. The most important thing is you, and I want you to remember that. Nobody can function if they are burnt out, and we want you to be the vest version of you that you can be. Some goals just take a little more time that others, and you will get there.

Finally, don't be afraid to pivot, even making changes at the last minute. Changing your way of working doesn't mean you've failed; it simply means you're being proactive and making better choices to bring your dream into fruition.

Amending a plan as needed is an essential aspect of achieving your goals no matter how big or small. Regular assessments, seeking feedback, being flexible, adjusting your requirements, and being proactive about making change can help you stay in charge of your life plan.

Reassessing And Adjusting Your Dreams

Reassessing and making changes your big dreams are an important part of the journey towards achieving your dream life. As you make progress towards your goals, it's natural to reflect on your your original dream concept and make tweaks as needed.

First, regularly reflect on your dream. Ask yourself if your dream is still relevant, if it aligns with your current values and priorities, and if it brings you joy and fulfilment. This self-reflection can help you determine if your dream needs to be changed, perhaps you think of it differently now, especially if a significant amount of time has passed since you first decided on it.

Next, seek out feedback from those closest to you. Talking to your family, friends, and support network can provide you with valuable overview and help you see your wants and needs from a different point of view. Perhaps you have been looking at things with rose tinted glasses and this could be the moment you truly open your eyes to the wonder of what you can truly achieve if you put your mind to it.

It's also important to be open to new experiences and opportunities. Sometimes unfamiliar experiences can broaden your horizons and lead to new discoveries that may change your take on things, therefore change your dream altogether.

Finally, don't be afraid to make these changes to your dream if needed. Your dream is a living and evolving goal, and making changes to it doesn't mean you have been unsuccessful, it simply means you're being astute and having awareness of how you truly think and feel. Your best life comes from what you need to be your true self and with time people change. What you needed then may not be what you need now. So do what's best for you and if in doubt go with your gut. Nothing is set in stone.

In conclusion, reassessing and adjusting your dream is a natural part of the journey towards achieving your aspirations. Regular reflection, seeking council, being open to new experiences, and being proactive about making changes can help you ensure your biggest dream aligns with your ultimate needs.

Reflection And Self-Evaluation

Reflection and self-evaluation are extremely valuable components of achieving your goal setting and goal completion. They provide opportunities for you to learn and grow as you progress, reflecting on the overall experiences, and make changes for the future.

First, regular reflection provides insights into your progress towards your mini goals. It allows you to see your successes and identify potential failures, identify areas for advancement, and make upgrades to your workflow to compensate if necessary.

Second, self-evaluation helps you understand your strengths and weaknesses. Self-evaluation helps increase self-awareness, enabling you to understand your thoughts, feelings, and behaviours. Having awareness of these traits can have a direct impact on how you work and you can compensate for this is needs be.

Third, reflection and self-evaluation can help you maintain a positive outlook and stay true to your beliefs. During this process you may find yourself of track for a number of reason, but being able to recognise this and lead yourself back to where you need to be is crucial to staying on task.

Finally, reflection and self-evaluation help you identify patterns. Look for times when you're most productive and identify the factors that contribute to your efficiency. These attributes should be factored into your action plans to help you make the best use of your time an energy when it comes to achieving your goals.

In conclusion, reflection and self-evaluation are crucial components of achieving your small goals and big dreams. They provide opportunities for you to gauge your performance, understand your virtues and vices, maintain a positive outlook, and fine-tune.

Setting And Achieving New Goals

Congratulations, you hit your goal! Now what's next?

Setting new goals is the next step of the journey towards achieving those big dreams.

Studies have shown that continuously setting new goals helps you maintain a growth mindset. This leads to increased resilience and determination. and helps you avoid complacency and stagnation.

Achieving a new goal provides a further sense of accomplishment and boosts your confidence even more. Each new goal you achieve is another step in the right direct, and can help take stock of your success.

As you achieve new goals, you acquire new skills and experiences, which can help you tackle new and even more challenging goals in the future. Once you get the first few under your belt you will eager to continue building a better life for yourself.

Setting new goals also provides opportunities to reassess your big dream. As you achieve your current mini goals and gain new experiences, you may find that your big dream evolves and changes, which is natural and normal. Use this chance the direction your life is heading and make and motions to realign thing if you need to.

Summary Of Key Points

The key takeaways from the book "Small Goals, Big Dreams" are:

1. Setting small goals is important in achieving big dreams as it helps break it down into manageable, achievable steps.

2. The benefits of setting small goals include increased motivation, focus, and a sense of accomplishment, which spurs you on.

3. Successful people have utilised small goals in their journey to achieve their big dreams and so can you.

4. Assessing your dream and breaking it down into smaller bitesize chunks is an important step in the process. Slow and steady wins the race!

5. Prioritising goal setting, creating a plan of action, and building a supportive network are crucial in achieving your goals.

6. Overcoming obstacles and setbacks, implementing a system of accountability, acknowledging progression, and staying on track are important strategies to help you get where you want to be

7. Reflection and self-evaluation, along with the ability to make changes to your plan, are perfectly normal. This is your life, make it how you want it.

8. Setting new goals is an important chapter of the achieving your biggest dream, as it helps you stay, focused, and allows you to continually grow and develop.

9. The journey towards achieving your goals and dreams is a continuous process, with opportunities for revision with the chance to live a life you love.

Final Thoughts

  The power of small goals in achieving big dreams is immense, and this book has aimed to highlight this concept and provide you with a roadmap for how to effectively utilise mini goals in you journey.

Small goals help us to break it down into manageable steps, which in turn helps us to stay focused and motivated. They provide a sense of accomplishment along the way and help us to build the skills and experiences we need to tackle any particularly challenging goals later on.

Moreover, small goals help us to stay accountable, build a supportive network, and overcome obstacles and setbacks along the way. They also provide opportunities for self-reflection, self-evaluation, and growth, as well as opportunities to reassess our dreams to being it inline with our current spiritual and physical needs.

The power of giving yourself small goals to achieve those big dreams lies in your ability to provide structure and direction to your aspirations, while also allowing you to evaluate the journey as you make it. With the right approach and mindset, small goals can help us achieve our big dreams in no time and live your most fulfilling life.

Reader Encouragement – Start Today

As the reader of this book, it is now time to take action and start setting those small goals towards any dream you may have. It is important to remember that the path towards your dream no matter how big or small starts with taking that first step and setting those first mini goals.

Remember that the plan you set today will help you build momentum and get closer to your dream with each passing day. And as you set and achieve your action points, you will develop the skills, experiences, and confidence you need to tackle increasingly challenging goals life may have for you.

Additionally, achieving those small goals will provide you with a sense of accomplishment and pride, as you see the progress you are making towards your best life. It will also provide opportunities for reflection, self-evaluation, and measuring your success.

In conclusion, the time to start on your path is now. Take that first step today and begin the journey towards the life you have always dreamed of. And always remember, the power of small goals in achieving big dreams is immense, and with the right approach and mindset, you can achieve anything you set your mind to.

I wish you every success with you dream, no matter what it may be. Rest assured you are in good company, and I believe in you.

Further Reading Recommendations

Here you can find a section dedicated to further reading recommendations. This section includes books that offer additional insights and perspectives on goal setting, motivation, and achieving success.

Some of the books recommended include:

"The 7 Habits of Highly Effective People" by Stephen Covey - This classic book provides a comprehensive overview of the habits and strategies that successful people use to achieve their goals.

"The Power of Intentional Leadership" by John C. Maxwell - This book explores the role of leadership in achieving success and offers practical tips and strategies for becoming a more effective leader.

"Mindset: The New Psychology of Success" by Carol S. Dweck - This book explores the importance of a growth mindset in achieving success and offers practical strategies for developing a more positive and productive outlook.

"The Compound Effect" by Darren Hardy - This book explores the power of small, consistent actions in achieving big results over time.

Goal Setting Breakdown And Example

Included in this book is a breakdown of the steps to follow in order to break down that big old dream of your into your small goals and get you started. I have also followed up the breakdown with an example so you can see how it would work in the real world.

- Define the larger goal: Start by clearly defining your larger goal. Make sure it is specific, measurable, attainable, relevant, and time-bound (SMART).
- Break down the larger goal: Break down your larger goal into smaller, manageable goals. These mini goals will serve as steppingstones towards achieving your larger goal.
- Assign deadlines: Assign a deadline to each mini goal to keep yourself accountable and on track.
- Create action points: For each mini goal, write down the specific actions you need to take in order to achieve it.
- Prioritise: Prioritise your mini-goals and action points, focusing on the most important ones first.

- Measure progress: Regularly measure your progress and make adjustments as needed. Celebrate your successes along the way.
- Reflect and adjust: Regularly reflect on your progress and adjust your goals and action points as needed.

Example:

The Dream:

"To increase my fitness level and run a 5K race within the next 6 months."

Small Goals:

- Start a regular exercise routine (deadline: 1 month)
- Increase running distance by 1 mile each week (deadline: 4 months)
- Complete a practice 5K race (deadline: 5 months)

Action Points:

- Start a regular exercise routine:
- Schedule time for exercise in your calendar
- Join a gym or fitness class
- Hire a personal trainer
- Increase running distance by 1 mile each week:
- Gradually increase running distance each week

- Seek advice from a running coach
- Join a running group

Complete a practice 5K race:

- Register for a 5K race
- Train for the race with the help of a coach or training program
- Complete the race and celebrate your success.

By following this template and breaking down your larger goal into smaller, manageable mini-goals and action points, you increase your chances of success and can achieve your larger goal.

Support And Guidance

In the UK, you can find goal-setting support through organizations such as the UK Career Coaches Consortium, the Career Development Institute, and the Institute of Career Guidance.

In the USA, organizations such as the National Career Development Association and the International Coach Federation offer support and resources for those looking to set and achieve their goals.

Whether you are looking for one-on-one support or simply seeking additional resources and information, the contact information provided in this book will help you find the guidance you need to achieve your big dream through small goals.

About The Author

 Olivia Murray is a renowned authority on Law of Attraction, self-love, and confidence. She is a multi-talented individual as a YouTuber, author, public speaker, and podcast host. Olivia's impactful work has transformed the lives of hundreds of thousands of people, helping them turn their dreams into reality.

She empowers women to trust their instincts and seize opportunities by taking charge of their lives. She inspires them to publish their own books, launch their own podcasts, host their own events, and design their lives to match their aspirations.

Olivia guides women entrepreneurs in refining their unique voice and becoming influential leaders in their respective fields. Her message of empowerment resonates with women from all cultures and backgrounds, breaking down barriers and promoting equal opportunities globally.

If You Enjoyed
This Book

Please consider leaving a review on Amazon!

As a self-employed, self-publishing creative, reviews are essential to get my content out for more people to enjoy.

Your review can make a huge difference!

Thank you for being here until the end, and keep your eyes peeled for my …

NEW BOOKS COMING SOON!